This book is dedicated to all those who make the world more beautiful.

ACKNOWLEDGEMENTS

These quotations were gathered lovingly but unscientifically over several years and/or contributed by many friends or acquaintances. Some arrived—and survived in our files—on scraps of paper and may therefore be imperfectly worded or attributed. To the authors, contributors and original sources, our thanks, and where appropriate, our apologies.
—The Editors

WITH SPECIAL THANKS TO

Jason Aldrich, Gerry Baird, Jay Baird, Neil Beaton, Josie Bissett, Jan Catey, Doug Cruickshank, Jim Darragh, Jennifer & Matt Ellison, Rob Estes, Michael Flynn & Family, Shannan Frisbie, Jennifer Hurwitz, Heidi Jones, Cristal & Brad Olberg, Janet Potter & Family, Diane Roger, Jenica Wilkie, Erik Lee, Heidi & Shale Yamada, Justi, Tote & Caden Yamada, Robert & Val Yamada, Kaz, Kristin, Kyle & Kendyl Yamada, Tai & Joy Yamada, Anne Zadra, August & Arline Zadra and Dan Zadra.

CREDITS

Compiled by Kobi Yamada and Kristel Wills
Illustrations & Design by Clarie Yam

ISBN: 1-932319-43-3

ISBN 1-932319-43-3   51495

7 49190 02828 8

9 781932 319439

Printed in China

And the day came when the risk it took to remain tight in the bud
was more painful than the risk it took to blossom.

ANAÏS NIN

Don't just go through life, grow through life. Don't just be good, be good for something and someone. Goodness heightens beauty. Become who you are, who you were meant to be. Seek out knowledge and experience. The more we see, the more we are capable of seeing. The more we do, the more we are capable of doing.

If you want change, begin it. If you want love, give it. If you want hope, embody it. Start immediately and do it flamboyantly. Once you've begun, don't turn back. Change and growth can be painful and challenging at times, but as Lauren Bond said, "Every flower has to go through a lot of dirt."

Life is about choices, growth and taking chances. It is about pushing through and moving forward. It is about loving courageously and not holding back. It is about finding a brighter, better way. You owe it to yourself and to the world to make the most out of the stuff that's in you.

Bloom into your incredibly, gloriously, brilliantly beautiful self. The world is waiting.

*There is only one time
when it is essential to awaken.*

That time is now.

BUDDHA

The flower has opened,
has been in the sun and is unafraid.
I'm taking more chances;
I'm bold and proud.

PAULA COLE

Even a thought,
even a possibility,
can shatter us
and transform us.

FRIEDRICH NIETZSCHE

We all have
the extraordinary
coded inside us,
waiting to be released.

JEAN HOUSTON

The journey between
what you once were
and who you are now becoming
is where the dance of life
really takes place.

BARBARA DEANGELIS

I will grow.

I will become something new and grand,

but no grander than I now am.

Just as the sky will be different in a few hours,

its present perfection and completeness

is not deficient, so am I presently perfect

and not deficient because

I will be different tomorrow.

WAYNE DYER

Face new challenges,
seize new opportunities,
test your resources against
the unknown and in the
process, discover your own
unique potential.

JOHN AMATT

*Another world is
not only possible,
she is on her way.*

On a quiet day,
I can hear
her breathing.

ARUNDHATI ROY

If a blade of grass springing up from a field has the

power to move you…rejoice, for your soul is alive.

ELEANORA DUSE

Beauty appears when something is completely and absolutely and openly itself.

DEENA METZGER

Not merely what we do, but what we try to do and why, are the true interpreters of what we are.

C.H. WOODWARD

You will either step forward into growth or you will step back into safety.

ABRAHAM MASLOW

The thing you are
ripening toward
is the fruit of your life.
It will make you
bright inside,
no matter what
you are outside.
It is a shining thing.

STUART EDWARD WHITE

It is only by following your deepest instinct that you can lead a rich life and if you let your fear of consequence prevent you from following your deepest instinct, then your life will be safe, expedient and thin.

KATHARINE BUTLER HATHAWAY

There is a place deep in your soul where a little seed rests. This seed is your amazing potential. Each time you push yourself, each time you breathe a true deep breath, each time you reach your hands to the stars, you nourish that little seed and feed your soul.

KAREN TYE

Growth itself
contains the germ
of happiness.

We ask ourselves,
Who am I to be
brilliant, gorgeous,
talented, fabulous?
Actually, who are you
not to be?

MARIANNE WILLIAMSON

A day dawns,
quite like other days;
in it, a single hour comes
quite like other hours;

but in that day
and in that hour
the chance of a lifetime
faces us.

MALTBIE BABCOCK

We do not believe in ourselves until someone reveals that something deep inside us is valuable, worth listening to, worthy of our trust, sacred to our touch. Once we believe in ourselves we can risk curiosity, wonder, spontaneous delight or any experience that reveals the human spirit.

E.E. CUMMINGS

If we could see the miracle
of a single flower clearly,
our whole life would change.

BUDDHA

Life is about becoming more than we are.

OPRAH WINFREY

If you were all alone in the universe with no one to talk to, no one with which to share the beauty of the stars, to laugh with, to touch, what would be your purpose in life? It is other life, it is love, which gives your life meaning. This is harmony. We must discover the joy of each other, the joy of challenge, the joy of growth.

MITSUGI SAOTOME

You learn to become optimistic by concentrating on things that give you

a sense of satisfaction, and you remain an
optimist by feeding those things to make them grow.

JURRIAAN KAMP

It is miraculous to see people change when they see they have choices. They open up like roses if they see they can make a difference — that they do have value.

BARBARA GLANZ

Love is the most difficult and
dangerous form of courage.
Courage is the most desperate,
admirable, and noble kind of love.

DELMORE SCHWARTZ

It takes a lot of courage to
release the familiar and seemingly
secure, to embrace the new.
But there is no real security in
what is no longer meaningful.

There is more security in the
adventurous and exciting,
for in movement there is life,
and in change there is power.

ALAN COHEN

Let us be grateful to
people who make us happy;
they are the charming gardeners
who make our souls blossom.

MARCEL PROUST

No creature is fully itself
    'til it is, like the dandelion,
opened in the bloom of
        pure relationship to the sun,
the entire living cosmos.

D.H. LAWRENCE